from there to here

michael mackmin

Happen*Stance*

Poems © Michael Mackmin, 2011
Cover image © Gillian Beaton, 2011
ISBN 978-1-905939-63-3
All rights reserved.

Acknowledgements:
Thanks are due to editors of the following publications, in which some of these poems first appeared: *Smith's Knoll, The SHOp, Seam, The Poetry Paper, The Rialto.*

Printed by The Dolphin Press
www.dolphinpress.co.uk

Published in 2011 by Happen*Stance*
21 Hatton Green, Glenrothes, Fife KY7 4SD
nell@happenstancepress.com
www.happenstancepress.com

Orders:
Individual pamphlets £4.00 (includes UK P&P).
Please make cheques payable to Happen*Stance* or order through PayPal in the website shop.

Contents

Here	5
The trap	6
Things fall apart	7
Her father	8
The word	10
The watchers	11
Flood	12
'When wheat is green, when hawthorn buds appear'	13
This poem explains	14
Then	15
Notes towards a September sonnet	16
Night piece	17
Lost (in transit)	18
December, for Lucy	19
The list	20
A thread	22
Interlude	23
The Aurelian	24
Him	25
Lamorna	26
Susannah	27
Sentences	28
These poems to	29
January 20th, 1986	30
Some deaths	31
There	32

for Ann

Here

This is an older landscape, smaller
fields, tufted copses, orchard plots
and each house has its vegetable piece—
the rows of beans, potatoes, clumps
of darker, large-leaved green where
squashes grow, swell yellow into
orange. At night, moths; in daytime,
bees (from their hive beside a stony
bank) work the flowers, while the ground
is populous with crickets, ants, hoppers,
flies. And in the walnut trees, a bird
hides, sings and hides again, unseen,
an unknown bird.

It was some such muck-and-wood-smoke-
scented farm Cincinnatus (remember him?)
quit, came back to, when he'd set
all straight, done his noble ancient Roman bit.

The trap

The heart trap
boxes me: I clump & thump
I cry my *yes*,
my anger bruised on walls.

Each atom in the iron
I love: watching
the falling sun.
The rot-choked fields unfold
ploughed clean at a whisper.

This is all,
this is all
you crooked broken
muscle &
flattered residence of love.

Things fall apart

White pick-up truck on the Cromer road
full of the naked dead: the driver
leans a long arm out to tip ash off
a cigarette, not indicate, but still
they go right at Alby Cross, down
towards the softer land. The road
ruts bounce and arms and legs begin,
end, embrace. Downhill then, where
Gary waits, JCB idling at the open trench.

A small way off, a girl on a horse sits
half hidden in the shade, hair
tied in a string of cloth. Lucy, who
yesterday was peeling stickers—hearts
and fairies, stars—onto 'I love you' notes
and is guard, a long gun resting
in the saddle holster. Meanwhile,
this burial done, the trucks turn back
for more. East there's smoke over Walsham—
the town taken and torched.
About time too, says Gary.

Her father

The old man loved wallflowers
the scent of them the mixed colour
for who knows why, maybe as I
treasure a particular crimson
rose because of you, Mel,
standing naked, wet, beside it.

His good daughter yearly
planted a bed of them, three
deep, against the house wall
so the windows, open, let the smell
colour the room. There's always
a good daughter, bad daughter

and maybe the same with sons: the
others are just 'the others' or
'the middle one'. Here
Melanie and Beth take,
resisting, but still take, those
roles. For Mel (the bad), Daddy

Dearest was not to be shocked, upset
(she did, of course). Beth, meanwhile,
sweating and sinking under her
goodness, looked after 'Father',
a man settled into oldness,
pink skin, bleach-white tonsure

and very clean clothes,
washed to an inch of their life.
Latin he'd quote. *Facilis
descensus Averno,* he'd say,
coming down the wide stairs
to breakfast with the family.

The word

As to why you come to see me Ms
Muse after so long and asking,
of all unlikely things, I get
a stick of seaside rock—pink
and white sweetness, apologising
(you!) for how you'd been. *Sorry,
keeping you at arm's length*,
giving, when I kiss, between the
freckles, a palest rose blush,
but it must have the right word.

And you standing then, tall on
your long legs, in the doorway
turning a little, looking back
dark pupils, a flicked smile
at the joke it all is, so funny
I can feel myself falling,
but it must have the right word.

And then, *Nice, but you know you need
three more lines, an ending, get
down to the seaside, shop for pink rock.*

The watchers

He slept among the nightingales,
pitched his tent in their glades,
studied their song. Noted how, first arrived
the amorous throb was loud-launched
skyward to ensnare the dawdling mate;

later softened, became chuckles
in the dark, merry music of desire—
she's mine, she's mine, yes, yes now
now and now. He wrote it down

drew graphs and spectograms, won
accolades (his praises sung). All gone:
the birds were trapped, their tongues
(O Philomel) torn out, stir fried
by TV chefs to tease the watchers' appetites.

Flood

A commonplace of dreams, it's said,
is that water (the lack, the excess)
stands in for feeling (the heart,
the gut, the genitals). A troubled
lake, much rain, a river brimming
foretell (backtell) ignored
stuff. Recognise, 'they' say, what's
left out (of your life) oh, *get
in touch*. It's that ah so sad
you don't know you're born therapy
horn.

And here's a child (1953) watching
water rise, one who, on safe ground,
sees the tide's fuller flow, knows
that, stubborn in the sea-wall houses,
some he loves hold out, as people do,
confident against harm—not
wanting to abandon carpets, cabinets
of Goss, pianos, things worked for—
when it's only sea and wind. And so
wolf water, cold and grim, goes
over, through, and the child
watches where they
drown.

'When wheat is green, when hawthorn buds appear'
A Midsummer Night's Dream, Act I, Scene i

Like the exact smell of a wet horse
hot after a canter: where were
you when the wheat was green?

Like the path edged with lavender and
the white pink *Mrs Simpkins*, where
were you when the hawthorn budded?

Oh we are all fed down tubes
by our mothers and when cut
away left with a knot in the
belly—just to remind us, just
to remind her, forget-me-not

like the blue of a mountain sky
glimpsed as cloud, swirled open,
closes. Sing of the heart when wheat

is green, being young, abashed
by love, and love, smiling,
stood at a Croydon

bus stop, the budded hawthorn
blistered, opened under
the whitest moon.

That painted galloper, time, has paced away
two thousand years: things, still,
are mostly made of tears.

MICHAEL MACKMIN

This poem explains

This poem explains the meaning of life,
especially for our time. I write
as my tutors here advise, of things
I know. They also say to *show not
tell*, which I also do. Philosophy
is my hobby, poetry my passion
as I'm sure you'll see. In stanza one
*the Picardy roses are sodden and spattered
in mud* refers to the First World War
and a popular marching song
then. However, it is a metaphor for all
the beautiful young men dead, donkeys
led by lions, as has been said.
In stanza two *the secret diarist
in her attic lair* refers to Anne
Frank who hid in an attic
and her family. Hitler wanted all Jews
dead and nearly succeeded. Some say
he is misunderstood but I think not.
The burning child who runs along the road
in stanza three refers to a photo
from the Vietnam war in black and white:
a naked child runs away from the war
and luckily was captured on film—
I explain the pity and terror.
In stanza four, *sponsored now
by Sky and CNN* is an original
idea of mine and Copyright—the idea is
that in our time the media will pay
for wars for people to watch. I hope
you like my poem. I hope you like my poem.

Then

Can be just a breath of air, warm, an
exact echo, turning a corner on a stone
path: the dark horizons, the one distant
light set going on its rock long passed
by Mr Stevenson. How do you show,
not tell, the first true love? That
downhill walk between stone walls, the
plaited wildflowers in our hair,
us singing hymns; rocks and stones,
the stony path, the night that's warm
when air is full of moths. Echo is and dies.
And someone counts the petals on those flowers,
their *loves me*, and their *loves me not*.

Notes towards a September sonnet

Mist on the sea and on the sea's
edge: adrift in silence the white
lighthouse, the black chimneys
on the lighthouse-keeper's house.
Inland is September blue. Westward
those journeys, seeking far islands
in green water, and love's comfort
(though her pale eyes slip sideways and
Sex she says, *give me sex don't talk to
me about love*. So, young, travelling on,
Yes I said *yes*). And what did we eat?
Sewin, grown fat in the estuary, gorging,
the fishermen claimed, on 'mollucs'; wiser
than salmon, big fish sliding along the water's bed.

Night piece

The mother says she saw the
                              crescent moon
and Venus, and as she walked
fireflies whizzed and burned.

So they waited. Saw the sunset's
                              fades
yellow through to flushed grey
                              then night

where hangs the toenail moon—
above, but nearer than, the hills—
(Venus is now a morning star).

Crickets, one nightingale in his
                              ancestral thicket
sings 'you, you, you, you, luck-luck, luck-luck'
                              O lovely

stars, another glass of wine. He says,
You know I love you.

No fireflies yet. They wait.

She turns to go. *I'm tired,* and then

the darkness blinks.

Lost (in transit)

Mike was thinking about Heavy
Houses—was sure the thought was
from, who? not him, he knew—and
how they flicked out darkness,
beams of it, deep and dazzling,
WARNING DANGER OF DEATH
like the pylon towers, their lightning
signs, or that notice of Deep Water.

Alison was in that seaside train
Hythe to Dymchurch, 1950s,
not sure if she wore a blue t-shirt,
yellow shorts or yellow shirt etc,
remembering being eleven. And talking
to a boy—how they spoke their names
but not their addresses. A conversation
and with a stranger—*we could be friends*.

They were not going to meet again: could
both be dead but were, as I write, not. Lost
from what might have been, traipsing
along, miles separate, lives filling
with longer sentences,
nothing on the telly, hell's
hot tongues licking at their feet. Brown
eyes and blue; knowing skin is under cloth.

December, for Lucy

Watching where a robin stood
and dipped to pick at little
bits of food where I'd been lumping
up and down, breaking wood

I thought about the goldfinch
that I took and cut
to see the heart, awed
how large it was in such a small—

yet capable for years, the flight,
the song, and yellowest of wings.
And this bird here, fat against
the cold, ticks, whirrs along—

singing is it? Is it singing
makes the heart get strong?

The list

The brushes (sable), the water colours,
the pastels, the blocks of paper,
the notebooks, the pencils, sharpened
just so, HB, B, 4H, the even, left
handed pencil sharpener, the italic pens,
the Rotring (™) pens, designer pens,
the stationery of blocked artistry,
the loose-leaf book, the ring-bound book,
books bought in Italy, in Ireland,
in France, the poetry of faint (feint?)
lines, of plain pages, the various and delicious
different weights of paper,
the undrawn, the unpainted, the unwritten
poem, the empty house, the dark
squares of its windows, the track down to it,
the Corsican pine, the five apple trees, the peach
still bearing wet fruit against the south wall,
the almond, the apricot, the black figs, the white
dust of the track, up the hill
the neighbour's thirty-nine hives,
the bees, the loud
buzzards' midday sunlit mew,
the bread on the table, the cracked
dish with the olives (black),
the white jug, the hard red
of the meat, the soft white of the cheese,
the lighting's illumination—death and
tomorrow—my beloved you, so
difficult to love, the grey road
under the grey tyres,
the shock, the sign, the breath

of dead poets which was their all,
our all, held in the air in this valley
where the eagle pauses, its
wings at the edge of a hover
looking for snakes, the locked
church, the roses yet budding
more red, more white, the unexamined life,
the mantis on the stone step,
the closed book, the door
latched with string, the four men
in the sunset bar, the cards in their hands.

A thread

Ann was dusting the apples.
Her daughter was having her
dressings changed, at the same time
wondering *was it worth it?*
They both wondered that—never
spoke it to the other though.
The bough had broken and Ann
had had to pick the apples,
piled them in bowls about the house,
more than I can ever eat.

The daughter said to her friend *but
I couldn't because of the child.*
And Ann said that too: it was a thread.
The men were banging the chimney about,
making it safe for winter. *Sorry,*
they said, *for all the dust.*

Interlude

We walked along a sunken lane, not
much travelled, grass in the centre,
found a tree rich in yellow fruit
ripe, so took and ate, gathered more.
Then the voice of the farmer in the
field above saying, *Good day*, asking
were we taking fruit?
Us, innocent
blatant, our hands behind our backs
full of soft figs, answering, *Yes.*
Take more, he says, *take more, eat.*

The Aurelian

The 'i' as she speaks it, is short, soft, as in
'sibling'. *Siberia,* she says, *I am from Siberia*—
a smile, blue jeans, blue eyes—a long journey
to come to be stood in a dented caravan, here
in the Marsham layby, selling asparagus,
'local' fruit, flowers (*You like? You want?*)—pale
skin, pale hair. *Here is small,* she says, thinks,
points to the glebe fields. *My country big.* Also,
*Here small streets, small houses, all small: first
I feel sick, but now I like.*

I catalogue blue butterflies to collect
the colour of her eyes: the upper wings,
Small Blue, Large Blue, Common Blue, the
Chalkhill Blue, Mazarin Blue, the Holly Blue
and, ah yes, you again, Adonis Blue—remember
that softest hair, the vulnerable abdomen,
and then the paler silvers of the underwing,
the wet brush, the painter dips and colours in.
What is your name? at last I ask. *Name?* she says.

Him

His heart hiccupped in his chest
like the lump of a pulse in a lizard's
neck. What of it? You about to write
a dead, a dying father poem?

Or remember him alive—the laugh,
in days when laughing men would
lift a knee and slap their thigh.
Then old Saunders said, the knee

lifts, *you don't look at the mantle-
piece when you're,* thigh slap, *poking
the fire!* And the laugh, bark,
bark, bark, the tear wiped away.

A good laugh, a hearty laugh. Those days
it was known, too, women, bless them,
didn't understand money—had it
counted out, the house-keeping,

kept it in purses. And a man, pleased,
shocked a bit, by some little woman's
cleverness, would crack a new note
at her, even once a white fiver,

say, *Here, buy yourself a new hat.*
She'd nag, he'd huff and cough: gone now.
The lizard on the step, bald eyes, flicked
tongue, that pulse bulging the body wall.

Lamorna

A boy in love with air, sea,
clambering on rocks, goes
higher, looks to the top, the blue:
finds himself in a stone fenced field
low plants in rows, violets, knows
this is where those bruised bunches
in the winter florists grow—
how someone on their knees in mud
nips and ties the stems. Violets, sweet
lovely violets, a posy for a long
legged boy to buy and say
Look mum I bought you violets.

The mother, in love with sunlight, lies
propped on her elbows, eyes the beach,
watches the rocks where, there he goes,
her funny boy, who kicked her heart,
who still kicks. His long legs take him
up, away, out of sight (never
out of mind), his first word *aeroplanes*
from when the bombers droned, the fighters
whined, fire falling from the sky.
What am I to do? What can I?
The string will snap between us and, oh
I have got a boy who brings his mother flowers.

Susannah

Is her face pale, or pale because she has
some skill in pallor? Some unguent, some
bottled moon? Or maybe the white is because
her black of hair, black of eyes, invents
white skin? My eyes are brown—
not as keen as once they were. And that's the why
of all I do is celebrate her round pale face,
her thin wrists stuck out of a dark jacket,
someone I'd once have called a 'girl'
standing, 8 pm, glass in hand,
being looked at in a bar.

Sentences

Blood in darkness spilt is black.

The gulls at dawn, fluttered to earth,
beating into wind.

The leaf, wet on earth, forms slowly into soil.

The voice, cluttered with certainty,
bites: I have the teeth marks inside.

Or,
or again alone & seeming desolately lost,
she asks.

At night in November a thin noise,
thrushes seeping through the dark:

in quiet further sound, frost and wings.

These poems to

These poems to myself, what is bitterness?
A juniper berry dries the mouth
anger and tears belched down
my belly a nest of it *how dare you die
how dare you leave?*

A slave suddenly free I stand
having to hold tight to me shackles
eyes down I gather
stones are cold jewels warm
salt pebbles to my mouth.

You are dead. I curl round you dead
never forgetting
I will never let you go
I have eaten your words, my bowels
do as you tell me to.

January 20th, 1986

Obsessed with grief, confused, midnight, I
set the kettle on the stove,
my mother's face my   mother   dying
There at last you have
your father has
a madwoman for a mother, she says
and smiles knowing she lies
a little white lie that harms nobody.

In the pain is an age of rage locked,
is you still locking in, your tears locked in;
they stay in their room waiting to learn
to be good.

Wet your eyes are but no further, no fall.
Men always win, you say,
mad at him, him all these years, lucid;
again I lock I lock myself out.

You sit and talk as if
nothing had happened nothing
is happening, your slow death.

Some deaths

What did the kind lady at the hospice say?
She said, *He had a good death*, she said—
her, her with the white Irish face, that
mop, puffed, fly-about hair, and the fingers,
the long bones there in her fingers, she said.

And the opposite? Is that a 'Bad Death', he had
'a bad death' ?
         No. Be quiet. 'Not a good death'
is the opposite. She'd rather always say, *He had
a good death*. And sometimes she has to take you
aside, into the room that's set aside, and sometimes
say it: *It was not A Good Death*, as if, Lucky you,
you missed it, it was not a good death, blood and shit
and shit, and blood, we held him down we shut
his mouth
he died.

THWACK! Like a mad daddy with his
swishing stick Death bangs the white light
into you: sudden. Or tricky comes with caress
and cuff, pinch and punch, seduces you with
stroke and kiss, and never, no O never says
*This, will
hurt me far more
than it hurts
you*. Good. Bad. Death dogs you.
Take the lead off its hook,
walk out into the woods.

MICHAEL MACKMIN

There
for Patrick

The distant hills are blue, purple,
dark as a bruise against the sky's
evening eye. From here to there is far—
a trouble, a journey not lightly taken,
things being as they are, the price
of wheat, the bigger field to plough.

So when he, the one traveller, came back, we
expected tales—got them: far other hills,
he said, lay westward, mountainous,
where lightning washes, glares,
and snow is permanent. Those who live
there murmur a beyond, but
things being as they are, the price
of wheat, the bigger field to plough,
it's not a journey any recommend.